Pelé

Soccer Legend

by Janet Woodward

SCHOOL PUBLISHERS

3 ©Getty Images; 4–7 Vasja Koman ©Harcourt Education Australia; 8–11 ©Getty Images; 12 ©CESAR FERRARI/Reuters/Picture Media; 13–14 ©Getty Images

Printed in China

ISBN 10: 0-15-351414-0
ISBN 13: 978-0-15-351414-2

Ordering Options
ISBN 10: 0-15-351212-1 (Grade 2 Advanced Collection)
ISBN 13: 978-0-15-351212-4 (Grade 2 Advanced Collection)
ISBN 10: 0-15-358049-6 (package of 5)
ISBN 13: 978-0-15-358049-9 (package of 5)

4 5 6 7 8 9 10   0940   15 14 13 12 11 10 09

Soccer legend Pelé is from Brazil, a country in South America. There were three children in his family. They lived with his parents, his grandmother, and his mom's brother.

The family was poor. This didn't stop Pelé from making his dream come true. He wanted to be a top soccer player, and he was.

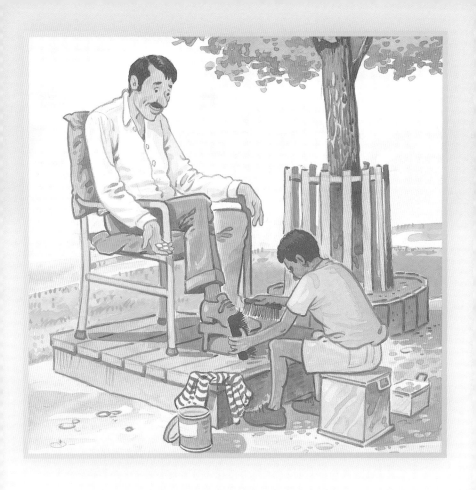

As a child, Pelé helped his uncle sell wood. Pelé also sold peanuts and shined shoes to make money. When he wasn't working, Pelé would play soccer with his neighbors. He was a wonderful player.

The neighborhood children played
in bare feet. They didn't always have
a soccer ball. Sometimes they had to
use a can, a grapefruit, a coconut, or
rolled up socks. This didn't matter to
Pelé though. He said, "Everything
is practice."

Pelé's father helped Pelé learn to play soccer. His dad had been a good soccer player. He had to give it up because of a knee problem. Like his dad, Pelé learned to knock the ball into the goal with his head.

Pelé once said, "Enthusiasm is everything." He had lots of enthusiasm for soccer.

In 1956, when Pelé was sixteen, his dream of being a soccer star started to come true. Pelé joined a top soccer team in Santos, Brazil.

Pelé (the third player from the left) with the Brazilian National soccer team in 1958

At eighteen, Pelé joined the army in Brazil for one year. He began playing soccer for an army team. Then he played for Brazil's national team.

The World Cup is the biggest prize in soccer. Pelé is still the only person who has played on three World Cup winning teams. He helped Brazil to win in 1958, 1962, and 1970.

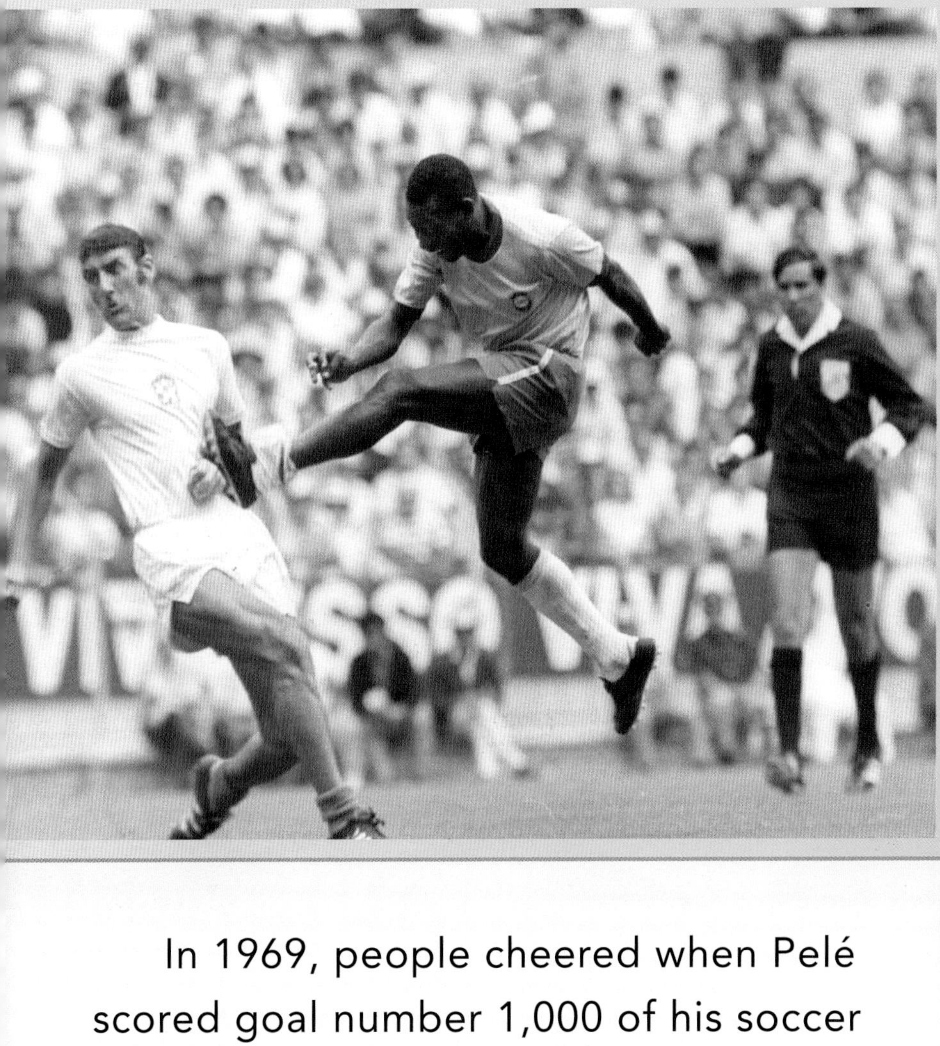

In 1969, people cheered when Pelé scored goal number 1,000 of his soccer career. This made him the player to score the most goals ever in soccer. Even today, no player has caught up with him.

Pelé has used his success to help other people. He has asked people to pay attention to the children of the world. He has helped raise a lot of money.

Today Pelé continues to raise money and help other people. He is Minister of Sports in Brazil. He helps soccer players and teams all over the country.

Pelé never gave up. His family didn't have much money, but he never lost sight of his dream. He always tried his best. That's what made him one of the world's greatest soccer players.